Nebuchadnezzar & Other Poems by Thomas Aird

Thomas Aird was born on 28th August 1802 at Bowden, Roxburghshire in Scotland.

After an education at the local parish school he studied for his degree at Edinburgh University. Whilst there he became friends with fellow writers James Hogg, Thomas Carlyle and John Wilson.

After graduating Aird was encouraged to become a Church of Scotland minister but he turned down these entreaties to remain in Edinburgh and devote himself to a literary career.

His first publication was in 1826 with 'Martzoufle: A Tragedy in Three Acts, with other Poems', unfortunately the collection received little attention from either critics or the public.

Aird was a regular contributor to Blackwood's Magazine and among other works a series of essays entitled 'Religious Characteristics'.

He was best known for his narrative poem 'The Captive of Fez' which was published in 1830 to a far better and wider reception.

Between 1832 and 1833, Aird succeeded James Ballantyne as the editor of the Edinburgh Weekly Journal. From 1835, he became the editor of the Dumfriesshire and Galloway Herald, a post he then held for the next 28 years. While editor, several of his poems were published within its pages.

In 1848, he published a collection of his poetry, 'The Old Bachelor in the Old Scottish Village', which was very well received. His friend, the essayist Thomas Carlyle, said that in his poetry he found "a healthy breath as of mountain breezes."

His last published literary work was his editing of the works of David Macbeth Moir, a physician and writer, in 1852.

Aird was to now concentrate on the editorship of the Herald until he retired in 1863.

Thomas Aird died on 25th April 1876 in Castlebank, Dumfries at the age of 73. He was buried at St Michael's Church.

Index of Contents

NEBUCHADNEZZER

Canto I

Cyra's Interview With The Prophet Ezekiel

I

To yon high hills, how fitly stern of stress,
Ezekiel takes the shattered wilderness,
Where rooted trees half hide, but not compose
To grace the births of Nature's rudest throes,
Imperfect, difficult, unreconciled:
Blind moaning caverns, rocks abruptly piled
Below, and herbless black peaks split asunder
Aloft, the awful gateways of the thunder,
Accord they not with him whose burdened eye
Sees, through the rent of kingdoms great and high,
Thick gleams of wrath divine, whose visions range
Throughout the obstructed solitudes of change,
Whose spirit stumbles 'midst the corner-stones
Of realms disjointed and of broken thrones?

II

As on Ezekiel strode, he saw a maid
Sit in the vale, and on a harp she played.
Before her state upon a rugged stone
A form of man, with tangled locks o'ergrown,
Haggard, and dark, and wild; of power and pride,
A milk-white horse was pawing by his side.
Near went the Prophet; up that savage man

Sprung, tossed his hair, and to the mountains ran;
O'er rocks and bushes bounding with him went,
With startled mane, that steed magnificent.
The minstrel rose; when she Ezekiel saw,
She laid her harp aside with modest awe;
In haste she came to meet him, named his name,
And prayed his blessing with a reverent claim.
"Maid, who art thou?"

"Cyra, of Judah I."
"Why dwelling here? And who yon form on high,
Chased by the mighty horse?"

"Thou man of God,
Austere thy visions, so is thy abode:
The stony mountains where old lions live,
Dread paths to thee, to thee a dwelling give:
Not in soft city, not in kingly dome
Thy jealous soul will deign to make thy home;
So art thou seldom within Babylon's gate,
And so hast heard not of her Monarch's fate,
Forth driven by God to wander from his throne,
Till seven appointed times be o'er him gone!
Behold that King—him followed by yon steed,
Doomed on the hills and in the wilds to feed!
His head forlorn, in nature's naked eye,
Is beat by all the changes of the sky;
He sees the morning star, and the wide noon,
He sees the nightly ordinance of the moon,
Sleep seldom his: The wild beast's in its den,
But through the night must roam the King of men!
Such was his sore extremity, till I—"

"So be abased—be stricken—worse than die,"
Exclaimed the Prophet, "who Jehovah's trust
Scorning, bow down our Zion to the dust!
So shall they be: Amazement shall lay bare
Her enemies' souls, and terror, and despair.
So has it been: Scarce Edom's name remains.
Soft Syria's loins are wrapped about with pains.
Tyre, where is she? The old haughty crocodile,
Is he not bridled on the shores of Nile?
On Ammon's head, on Moab's, Jehovah's doom
Has poured a midnight of unmelted gloom!
God is gone forth! Abroad His swift storms fly,
And strike the mystic birds from out the sky:
Soar proudly, burnished birds of Nineveh,
Home to the windows of your glory flee;

Ha! broke your wings, your trodden plumage rots—
The doves of Ashur lie among the pots!
For him! for yonder outcast—wo! and wo
Still more to him who thus has brought her low!—
Beneath her branchless palm must Judah sit,
Her widowed face with pens of sorrow writ,
And round her feet the fetters! But has he
Reaped glory hence? Earth's proud men, come and see!
At best a royal brute, he even without
The majesty of mischief roams about!
So let him—"

"Whelmed beneath Jehovah's ban,
'Tis ours to spare the much-enduring man.
Sore laid on us, his hand crushed down our State;
And great the blame, as our oppression great:
Yea, curse his pride of warlike youth; Oh then,
Still let me name him 'midst earth's noblest men!
But he was bowed, and, prostrate in his change,
Followed the wild ox in his boundless range,
And ate the grass; his head was wet with dew;
Like claws his nails, his hair like feathers grew.
But I have helped him through his years of ill,
And ne'er will leave him, but will love him still.
Bless him, and curse him not!"

With anger shook
The son of Buzi; tragic waxed his look;
With vehement force, as if to meet the storm,
He wrapped his rugged mantle round his form.
"Look to me, damsel!" cried he: "are not we
Carried away by our iniquity?
Shall then the soft desires of woman rule
Thy spirit still, and make thee play the fool?
Because within his silken palaces
He made thee dwell in love's delicious ease,
Thou thought'st it good, and chased him to the hill
In caves of rocks to play the harlot still?
Lord God of Israel! shall we count it light
So to be driven from Zion's holy height,
Our princes captives made, our stately men
Hewn down in battle, Thy dread courts a den;
And scorning types without, and rites within
Of penitence, conform to Heathen sin;
No thought of our estate, no sigh for it,
Degrading even the dust wherein we sit?
Happy the slain ones of our people! blest
Who fell in Zion's wars, and are at rest!

Yea, happy they whose shoulders labour sore,
With burdens peeled, or weary with the oar;
For so their manly bodies are not broke
With idle dalliance—slavery's heaviest yoke!
Ye tall and goodly youths, your fate is worse,
Your beauty more than burning is a curse;
For ye must stand in palaces, soft slaves
Of kings—your brethren lie in noble graves!—
Until your base shame for your origin
Beyond your wanton masters make you sin;
For ye upon the mountains, with desire
Unholy, looking toward the Persian fire,
Eat, not Jehovah-ward, forgetting Him,
Forgot the gates of old Jerusalem!—
Thou, too, thou maid of Judah, wo! that thou
Hast lived to be what I must deem thee now!"

He ceased. Like flames that burn the sacrifice
With darting points, shone out the virgin's eyes;
Shook her black locks of youth; drawn back she stood
Dilating high in her indignant mood.
She seized her harp, she swept the chords along,
Forth burst a troubled and tumultuous song;
Till, purified from anger and from shame,
Austere, severely solemn it became;
Yet dashed with leaping notes, as if to tell
Jehovah mighty for His Israel.
Soft gleamed the Prophet's eyes; he knew that strain,
Heard in the days of Salem's glorious reign,
When Judah's maids in sacred bands advanced,
With garlands crowned, and to the timbrel danced.
And shone through glazing tears young Cyra's eyes,
Her forehead now uplifted to the skies.
Her harp she dropped; her bosom greatly heaved,
Till words burst forth, and thus her heart relieved:—
"Perish the song, the harp, the hand for aye;
Die the remembrance of our land away;
Ne'er be revived the praises of the Lord
In the glad days of Zion's courts restored,
If I—" again she sobbed and hid her face—
"If I have been the child of such disgrace!
But ah! forgive me, great Ezekiel,
Thus to be angry I have done not well;
For thine the spirit that for Israel's weal
Burns with the fires of jealousy and zeal.
Oh hear thy handmaid now! for I shall sleep
In death, ere cease I for yon King to weep.
In that dread night—his wars be judged by God!—

When o'er our walls victoriously he rode,
He saw me lying in the trampled mire,
Which bloody glittered to the midnight fire;
Sprung, snatched me from my mother's dead embrace,
Ere the fierce war-steeds trode my infant face;
Smiled on me; to his large mailed bosom pressed me;
Home took me with him, with his love caressed me,
There made me dwell, there gave to me a name,
And to me there a father all became.

"Then—for my sacred origin I knew—
Me, yet a child, Jehovah taught to view
With scorn the Gentiles' sins; my opening days
Taught, more than theirs, to love our people's ways.
The Monarch smiled: nor sought he to subdue
The spirit honoured whence my choice I drew;
He gave me Hebrew teachers, them he charged
To see my childhood with their lore enlarged,
To compromise not in their captive place,
But tell Jehovah's doings for our race,
The ancient glories of our people tell,
And in his Court like princes made them dwell.

"Nor heavier task was mine, than that the King
A song of gladness made me often sing,
To cheer his spirit; for Jehovah vexed him
With nightly visions, and with dreams perplexed him.
My harp I touched; when he was cheered, then I
The mournful hymns of our captivity
Did ne'er forget: magnanimous he smiled,
And called me playfully an artful child;
Then was I bold, my prayer he heard with grace,
And gravely promised to restore our race.
God cast him out; I followed to the hills
My more than father, to divide his ills:
On summits high, and in the wastes his lair,
I found him strange and brutish in despair;
But tried my harp, less savage soon he grew,
And softly followed through the falling dew.
Caves in yon rock, our mountain people there
Had helped me first his dwelling to prepare;
There now less wild the food of men he finds,
And lies through night unstricken by the winds.

"In yonder hut a shepherd of our race
For years has given me an abiding-place.
His daughters love me as their sister; they
My simple service share with me by day,

To feed the flocks. When men their labour leave,
And past is now the milking-time of eve,
I harp before his cave, down from the steep
Comes the wild King, and couches him to sleep—
Oh, not to sleep; with self-accusing blame,
With madness wrestling, and with fitful shame.
Sweet psalms I play him then, till in calm wo
Lies his large heart; then to our cot I go.

"By Daniel's wise advice, his battle-steed
Was brought beside him on the hills to feed;
His armour too was brought, before his eyes
Nightly it gleams as on his bed he lies:
Memorials these of his heroic days,
To deeds of men again his soul to raise.
Remembering hence his glory, more because
The appointed season to a period draws,
His heart with reason swells; his ancient men
Of counsel come to seek him in his den.

Taught by affliction, by our God restored,
Then will he free the people of the Lord.
'Joy! joy for Zion!' let the captives sing.
Come thou with me, oh come and bless the wandering King!"

"True child of Judah! by the Spirit's might
Drawn to those hills, I wait the visioned night.
Just is thy gratitude. The God of peace
Raise up the King, and make our bondage cease!
My thought injurious turns to solemn praise;
And if thou keep thy sweet unblemished days
In Heathen courts, and if thy gentle power
May for our people haste redemption's hour,
Praised shalt thou be in Israel's borders wide,
Yea, praised—be this thy just and awful pride—
In Heaven, where the great Sanctities abide."

So spake the Seer. Low bowing to be blest,
The Jewess knelt; stooping her head he kissed,
Then turned away; with sobbing joy o'ercome,
Thus well approved, the virgin sought her home.

Canto II

The Plot Of Merdan And Narses

High rides the summer moon: Away, how slow,
The lordly waters of Euphrates go!
But see! a shadowy form from yonder rank
Of glimmering trees comes o'er the open bank.
Here Narses meets him:—"Merdan, you are late."
"Admit the toils that on my office wait,
And say, your purpose."

"Nay, 'tis mine to hear
What first you promised to my midnight ear."
Then Merdan spake:—"Our mutual hearts are known,
Why pause we then? Our theme be now the throne.
Meet we not here on our appointed way,
To learn from Chardes what the planets say,
Who nightly standing on his glimpsing towers,
With piercing ken looks through the starry hours?
Not rivals, twins are we in present sway;
What then? 'tis based upon the passing day.
Can we maintain it? Merodach is weak:
His father now those ancient servants seek:
Reason returns: again he'll sit on high:
And with our lives the Prince his own mean life will buy."

"Ha! yes; he knows his feebleness has failed
To back our counsels: these shall be assailed:
The blame of his misrule must we exhaust;
And, if we live, our power at least is past."

"His faith, nor might, to us can safety bring:
Who trusts him hides his jewel in a sling.
In heart he is a parricide, but still
His weakness fears to justify his will.
May such be trusted? Not his innocence;
He must be guilty, for our hope is thence.
'Tis ours to goad him on to such a length,
That farthest crime alone may seem his strength."

"Say we at once the outcast Monarch slew,
And crushed our fears?"

"Nay, that his son must do;
So shall our knowledge of his guilt ensure
Bribes for our silence, and our rule endure.
Well, then, at once, he must insult his sire,
That fears for life may perfect his desire,
And thus complete the parricide. On high,
Where vales embosomed in the mountains lie,
I know a place where comes the desert King

Each noon his limbs beneath the shade to fling.
Beside him feeds his battle-horse, that bore
His youth triumphant on from shore to shore,
A prince's gift, much loved: Near couched each night,
Upsprings he neighing with the morning light,
Awakes his lord, again goes forth with him
To range the pastures till the twilight dim.

"Now Parthian Chud's our friend, advanced by us
To keep the royal hounds, he'll help us thus:—
His tiger-dogs, from India's northern woods,
Fell mountain-climbers, glorying in the floods,
Three previous days shall hunger, till arise
Their bristly necks, and burn their lamping eyes;
Then shall our Monarch hunt; they, famine-clung,
Shall sweep the barren hills with lolling tongue,
Where no prey is, led thither on pretence
That there 'twas seen—it since has wandered thence.
Chud then, instructed, shall his Sovereign lure
To nearer hills, as if it there were sure;
And in the noon shall he his beagles lead
To where the wild King loiters with his steed.
Behold them started! Rush the kindled pack;
Not even unfeigned restraint could keep them back,
So fiercely hunger pricks their headlong way,
Against their instinct on the unwonted prey.
Onward they drive: At once, perhaps—'tis well—
The Ox-King falls before their crowding yell;
Nor bone, nor scalp, the bloody grass alone
Next moment tells our fears with him are gone.
If Chud from royal game can them restrain,
At least on Zublon shall they go amain;
Or falls the horse, or flees but soon to fall.
The mad King sees his son—has seen it all.

That son away pursues the storm of chase,
And ne'er again dares see his father's face.
What must he do? The rest has been explained:
His sire must die: Our place is thus maintained."

"This more: Our King, when Prince, with bold desire
Loved Cyra, heedless of his angry sire.
When Heaven's decree against the latter sped,
The Hebrew damsel from the Palace fled.
But I have learned her haunt; far in the wild
She dwells, a Jewish hind's adopted child,
The embruted Monarch near; for hers the praise
To love, to tend him through his humbled days.

So let this maid be carried from her place,
Say on the night of our appointed chase;
Then, for I know our Sovereign loves her still,
Shall she become the creature of his will.
Then, in his hours of hope unfilial
And mingled fear, shall we declare her thrall—
Thus from the service of his father gained
By force, and in his palace thus detained.
So shall he feel again that father wronged;
And dare be bold, to have his life prolonged."

"Our scheme is doubly one, how wisely blent!
It but remains to push it to the event.
This be in haste, for Persia's threatened war
Against us hangs upon the east afar.
The issue? Good our plan in any case.
But now our King has leisure for the chase."

"Behold! the first faint shoots of morning light
Breathe upward through the shadowy cone of night,
Sickening the eastern stars: 'Tis now the time,
Old Chardes waits us on his watch sublime;
From him the signs celestial shall we know,
Shape farther plans, and onward safely go."

Canto III

The Hunt

Before her cavern stands at evening-tide
Cyra, her harp clear glittering by her side;
Now for the King she looks far east away,
And now she turns unto the setting day;
She veils her dazzled face, her garments shine
With molten gold, like angel robes divine,
Touched by the sun, as large he stoops to rest
Beyond the Assyrian kingdoms in the west.
Eastward again she looked: she cleared her eye—
Ha! yes, she sees come o'er yon mountain high
A courser white; swift dogs are on his rear;
Upcoming hunters on the hill appear.
Can that be Zublon? From the mountain fails
The chase now swallowed by the nearer vales,
Perplexed and wide; again it comes in sight,
And lo! 'tis Zublon sure that leads the flight.
He takes the river, stems it with disdain,

Paws the near shore, forth springs, comes on amain.
The yielding dogs float down athwart the flood,
Swarm on the bank, renew their yells for blood,
Regain their track; inextricable, dense,
With crowding heads they wedge their way intense.
In fear majestic on the charger drew;
White clouds of smoke his seething nostrils blew;
Now streamed his tail on high, now swept the plain;
Abroad were driven the terrors of his mane.
He toiled, he strained, he neared the well-known maid,
He saw his rock, turning he proudly neighed,
Went reeking past, and rushed into his cave;
And Cyra ran the gallant horse to save.

Quick dipped in oil, and lit, in either hand,
Of gummy pine she bore a waving brand,
Forth held them, hasted to the entrance back,
There met the brindled leaders of the pack,
Scorched their dry tongues, and blinded them with fire,
And still she kept them back, still forced them to retire.
One minute more! impelled by crowding power
And hungry rage, the damsel they'll devour.
But here be mountain woodmen; they have heard
The tumult, hasted, and the maid will guard,
True to the King: with banded axes they
Dashed off the dogs, and kept them still at bay,
Till Chud the hunter came with smarting thong,
And down the mountain lashed the yelling throng.

Canto IV

Nebuchadnezzar's Cave

I

The moon full-orbed came up the east, and shone
Sweetly above the hills of Babylon:
Forth went the virgin Cyra by her light,
And wet her sandals in the dews of night,
Oft pausing she to strike her harp's clear string,
Through the still vales to lure the homeward King.
Long hours she roamed, but ne'er her wild lord came;
The keener heavens breathed chilly through her frame;
Then back she slowly went, and, to divide
The lonely hours, her scented fire supplied.
Nor yet, her hope though fainting, did she leave

Undone the filial duty of each eve;
But mixed his bowls of milk and tempered wine,
With drops infused, the pith of flowers divine,
In gentle wisdom that their healing dew
In nightly sleep his spirit might renew.

II

A foot, a shadow came; uprose the maid;
'Tis he!—forward she springs—is she afraid?—
Awed she draws back, she stands in mute surprise,
To see that solemn light within his eyes—
The strict concentred check—the lucid reins
Of reason, ruler o'er ecstatic pains.
With silent love on Cyra long he gazed,
Till came some quick sense of his life abased;
Gleamed his proud tears; into his cave's recess
He turned away in his sublime distress,
As in pale Hades, 'midst dim-visioned things,
Stalk the proud shadows of forgotten kings.

III

Her lamp the maid replenished with the oil
Of fragrant trees, to work a pleasing toil
Of needlework. Too glad for this, she stood
Entranced, till startled by a groan subdued.
Noiseless her footsteps as the falling snows,
With shaded lamp unto the King she goes;
Lets fall the shifting light by mild degrees,
Till now the features of her lord she sees.
He sleeps, yet brokenly; those sultry gleams
Betray a spirit toiling in his dreams.
Forth Cyra hastes, but soon she reappears
With mingled balms; with these, and with her tears
That dropped the while, she washed those dews away
From off his forehead, till refreshed he lay;
And kissed his cheek, and with a daughter's care
Arranged the masses of his raven hair.

IV

Then sate the maid, unrolling, white as milk,
Down from her knee a web of Persian silk,
Flowered by her needle, as her shaping mind

A second, third!—oh, how may she escape?

She starts—she's seized—she struggles—shrieks for aid,
In vain; the King in charmèd sleep is laid.
Masked forms around her throng, with many a foot
The emblazoned web of beauty they pollute.
Even Zublon's help she craves in her dismay;
But yielding, fainting, she is borne away.

Canto V

The Battle

I

Forth flames the day. From off his terrace high
The King Chaldean, with a troubled eye,
Long eastward looks; for lo! afar descried,
Comes on the Persian war sun-glorified,
To quell his throne. His nearer view commands
The embattled might of Babylonian lands,
In gorgeous ferment. From the city pour
Fresh hosts continuous through the impatient hour:
Their jostling chariots leap; the tide runs high
With all the pomp of flowing chivalry,
Arabian camels, and Nisæan steeds
Bearing a province of auxiliar Medes.
Onward they scour; for westward o'er the plain
The flower of Persian kingdoms draws its train,
From where its world of waters Indus brings
To Ocean, upward by his hoary springs,
To where the Tartar's winking hordes look forth
Over the snowy bastions of the North—
An army great and terrible: Earth seems
To be on fire beneath their brazen gleams.

II

Near waxed the fronting lines; intensely keen
They paused: stern was the silence them between.
Loud blew the Persian trumpets, wide the heaven
By one great shout from all their hosts was riven.
Chaldea answered on the west. At once
The Immortal Band of Persia's youth advance,
Flanked by a cloudy stir on either side,

Of swarming horse and archers opening wide.
Came o'er each army, darkening like a shroud,
The crossing texture of the arrowy cloud.
Beneath, the vans were locked together grim,
Were interfused the battle's ridges dim,
There opening, closing here, till form gave way,
Forgot the imposing beauty of array.

How gazed the King, intensely forward bowed,
As thick and thicker grew the battle-cloud,
Still darker waxed, now broke in lightened seams,
Again devoured the momentary gleams!
Forth rushed a western wind, backward it rolled
The heavy battle's slow uplifted fold.
O beauty terrible! he saw afar
The sultry ridges of the heaving war,
Saw down long avenues of disarray
The harsh-scythed chariots mow their levelled way.
'Twas doubtful long, but now the struggle pressed
With weight slow-whelming, gaining on the west;
Far back are swayed the wide Chaldean swarms,
They bow, they faint before the Persian arms.
But hark! a mighty trumpet in the west!
But lo! a warrior for the combat drest
In mail refulgent, on a milk-white steed,
Comes dashing east with earth-devouring speed!

Started the Prince, pale grew his forehead, shook
His knees, as stood he still constrained to look;
For, ha! his father's form that champion showed,
And plunging deep into the battle rode.
Far waved his sway, stemmed the Chaldean rout,
And changed their terror to a mighty shout,
By thousand thousands on the turrets thronged,
And lofty walls of Babylon, prolonged.
A sultrier ferment stirred the field: a band
Thickened behind that arm of high command,
As onward, eastward, with the whirlpool's might,
It sucked the reflux of the scattered fight;
Till, with its full concentrated attack,
It bore the centre of the Persians back.
Nor this alone: in shouldered masses wide
Their van was cleared away on either side.
And deep was pushed that column unwithstood,
And aye that waste collateral was renewed,
Till eastward far the Babylonian host
More than regained the ground which they had lost.
Then reeled the Persian power; it wavered, broke,

Was it not Thou? Brightness was Thy attire,
Mild walking with them on the stones of fire!
Under Thy dread permission, in Thy sight
I rise a King; but I will reign aright.
Though greatly wronged, to-day though galled my pride,
Yet to my heart shall vengeance be denied.
Yea, by their insults of this day extreme,
My foes have chased my madness like a dream.
Theirs no excuse; yet, by Thy grace upraised,
To me Thy mercy shall by mine be praised:
For I am humbled; ne'er shall be forgot
Thy power which curbed me down to such a lot.
Oh hear me now for her, this precious child,
More than my daughter on the mountains wild!

For me her dear eyes faint: Great God of Heaven,
Be health, be gladness to my Cyra given!
Let her but live, that I to her may prove
At least a father for her boundless love!"
He ceased. Young reverence her eyes abased;
With trembling joy a cup to him she raised.
He took the cup, with murmured love he blessed
The virgin, drank, retired, and lay at rest;
For she had spiced it with the sovereign flowers
Of sleep, to soothe him through the midnight hours.

VI

There sits young Cyra! As her work is sped,
Waves the redundant glory of her head,
Her dark and heavy locks. Oh, more than wife!
Oh, bold and lavish of thy generous life
For him thy lord! What though, by cares subdued,
Pale is thy cheek, O virgin greatly good,
All fair art thou as the accomplished eve,
Whose finished glories not a wish can leave;
Yea, more than eve consummate, as her skies
Where lurk the cognate morrow's glorious dyes:
So wears thy youth still promise, still when won
The perfect grace of every duty done!
Yea, who can see thee in this holy hour,
Nor deem thee guarded by supernal power?
Nor deem he sees, of Watchers here divine,
Incessant gleams around this cavern shine?
Light speed thy task, young Cyra; happy be;
Here angel wings are visitant for thee!
But hush! but hark! ha! see—a stealthy shape!

Thereon the King's young conquests had designed,—
From Nile victorious to the glimmering North,
Whose pictured form with keys of ice came forth;
O'er Tyre triumphant, o'er Damascus, o'er
Great kingdoms eastward to the Indian shore:
All here portrayed in glory and in gloom,
Rich as the work of an enchanted loom.
Her heart a silent covenant had made,
The finished gift before him should be laid
That solemn day, when he should leave that den,
Raised up by God again to govern men;
That to his heart, his humbled sense, his awe
Of Him who ruled him with a wondrous law—
His fear from this—his joy, redeemed—his thought
Of her who loved him, and that picture wrought,
A lasting great memorial it might be,
That Zion's captives he was bound to free.
His reason comes, her half-wrought cloth demands
The sleepless haste of her unwearied hands.

V

Forth came the King; his worn and awful face,
On Cyra bent, began to melt apace
To gleams—how tender! farther still subdued
To mingled tears of more than gratitude.

Stung by some fierce remembrance, fiercely changed,
With sudden strides throughout the cave he ranged;
Like toil-caught lion of his prey bereaved,
The mighty hinges of his bosom heaved;
Wild flew his locks; and darkness o'er his face
Settled, like night upon the desert place.
But trembling came: he knelt with humbled brow,
Solemn as when the ancient forests bow,
Smote by the cardinal winds:—"I know Thee well,"
Uprising, said he, "God of Israel!
The bright stars are the dust beneath Thy feet!
Vast ages dim not Thine essential seat!
Yet these permitted eyes, did they not see
Thy Glory in the furnace with the Three?
An effluence, like a globe of crystal air,
Was round about them: scathless was their hair.
Beyond, the red and roaring haze but showed
More beautiful these children of their God.
A Fourth was with them: glowing were His feet
As iron drawn from out the boiling heat!

Was forced, was whelmed in one commingled shock.
Their camels fled, their Indian archers ceased,
Their chariots rolled away into the east;
Far driven their host, consumed, like stubble sere
Wide fired when withering east winds close the year.

III

The Prince his chamber sought: he bade with speed
Narses and Merdan come, his counsellors of need.
They came. "We task you not," he cried, "to say,
Not even to guess that Victor of this day.

Slaves! slaves! we'll hear you not. This night at least,
This one night more, we'll be a king and feast.
Our Palace guards be doubled. Then when we
Are flown with cups, and filled with midnight glee,
Be Cyra brought; we'll make her drink old wine,
Her heart to warm, to make her beauty shine:
Long have we loved her; and, by Bel above!
Ere morn shall we be happy in her love."

Canto VI

The Banquet

Come to the Banquet! Lift your dazzled eyes,
Survey the glory that before you lies!
Far down yon avenue of fainting light,
The dim dance swims away upon the sight.
Behold the central feast! Behold the wine
Around in brimming undulations shine,
As shakes the joyous board! There Beauty sips
The purple glimmer with her murmuring lips;
For there the rose-crowned concubines are set,
For there the nymphs of Babylon are met,
Each one a princess: Their illumined eyes
Glitter with laughter, glance with coy surprise;
And aye the love-sick dulcimer is played,
Till faintly languishes each melting maid.
Here peaceful satraps quaff: their lordly breasts
Built out with gladness, sit the chosen guests.
And there the Prince: But oft he looks around,
And seems to listen for some coming sound.
Fear in his heart; each bowl, each golden cup

With blood, for wine, to him seems welling up,
Smote by the light of that branched candlestick:
These Holy Vessels well may make him sick,
Torn from Jehovah's Courts with impious hands,
To light the unhallowed feasts of Heathen lands.

II

But see young Cyra brought by eunuch slaves,
Pale, pale as are the dead within their graves,
Yet beautiful, in vestments flowered and fair,
With hasty garlands in her raven hair.
Pleased are the nobles of the banquet; round
Soft murmurs tell the favour she has found.
'Gainst scorn and wrong her heart had high defence;
Approval quelled her glowing innocence,
And Cyra tore the roses from her head,
In trembling haste her Jewish veil to shed.
It was not there; but nature there supplied
More than the wimple of a regal bride,
How lovelier far! Her eager hand unbound
Her hair dishevelled; far it fell around
Her comely form, black as the ancient Night,
And veiled the virgin from that insolent light.

Entranced in love, forgetting every fear,
And flushed with wine, the reeling Prince drew near.
"Thou chosen flower of Jewry, why so pale?"
He cried. "Nay, look from out that envious veil.
Give me thy soft hand, come drink wine with me,
Cling to my love, my bosom's jewel be!"

Back Cyra stepped, her tresses back she threw;
Their wavy beauty o'er her shoulders flew.
But burned her eye intense, as far it looked,
Nor check of terror intermediate brooked;
For in a moment the prophetic might,
God-given, was hers, the seer's awful sight.
Pale, fixedly rapt, concentrated, entranced
She stood, one arm outstretched, one foot advanced;
Nor moved that foot, nor fell that arm disturbed,
Not for a moment was her far glance curbed,
As from her lips, o'erruled with Heavenly flame,
The impetuous words that told the vision came:—
"Cling to thy love? I see a haughtier bride
Sent down from Heaven to clasp thy wedded side!
Oh, more than power, than majesty she brings,

Drawn from the loins of old anointed Kings,
To be her dower! Destruction is her name,
With terror crowned, with sorrow and with shame!
Her eyes of ravishment shall burn thee up!
And Babylon shall drink her mingled cup!
Weary thine idol-gods, old Babylon;
Yet tremble, tremble for thy glory gone!
City of waters! not o'erflowing thee,
Thy boasted streams shall yet thy ruin be!
Look to thy rivers! Shod with crusted blood,
The Persian mule—I see him on thy flood
Walk with dry hoof! Ha! in thy hour of trust,
He stamps thy golden palaces to dust,
Which dims the bold winds of the wilderness
One hour—Then, where art thou? And who shall guess
Thy pomp? its place, even? Let the bittern harsh
Give quaking answer from her sullen marsh;
From drier haunts, where doleful creatures dwell,
Let tell the satyr, let the dragon tell!"

She ceased, she clasped her hands, nor yet withdrew
Her eye concentred in its piercing view.
"Nay," said the Prince, "it ill befits those lips
To talk of kingdoms' and of thrones' eclipse!

Rein now the lovely madness of those eyes,
And see the bliss that near before thee lies.
Thy harp? 'Twas fetched with thee from out the cave."
—The Monarch nodded to a waiting slave,
The harp was brought—"Now, strike one nuptial strain
Of those that graced thy wisest Sovereign's reign:
Sing a glad song of Solomon." She took
Her harp inviolate, as with scorn she shook;
Forth, burst on burst, her holy quarrel leapt
'Gainst Zion's mockers, as the chords she swept.
"Nay," cried the Prince, and interposed his hand,
"Sweet Fury, stay; thy harp must be more bland.
Give us—we'll teach thee." Back in sacred pride
The Jewess shrunk. "It shall not be!" she cried.
"Our people's woes—O Jacob's God, how long?—
Have filled these chords with many a mournful song,
Have sanctified them thus. Yea, for thy King,
Thy father, too, how oft has thrilled each string,
To soothe him in the lonely wilderness,
By thee forgotten in his sore distress!
But I did ne'er forget him! Thou bad son,
My harp were tainted, touched by such a one,
Ungrateful, daring in voluptuous rest,

In the flowered garments of thy women drest,
To shame the throne of such a father; yea,
With dogs of chase to vex him in thy play!
Ne'er shall thy finger touch one hallowed wire!"
Mighty beyond herself, in holy ire
She burst the chords, her harp asunder tore,
And wildly strewed the fragments on the floor.

In quick revulsion kneeling down she cast
Her eyes to Heaven. Loud blew a trumpet blast.
Up sprung she. Fear was in the Prince's eye;
Yet, "To my chamber with her!" was his cry.

Slaves seized the maid; she shrieked; with effort strong,
Oh, minutes, moments could she but prolong!
Hark! shouts and clashing swords!—"Help, God, ere I
Must—" is she saved? The doors wide bursting fly;
He comes sublime—'tis he! the King restored!
Faces and forms of war dread thronging guard their lord.

Canto VII

The Death Of Cyra

"Majestic child of gratitude! this hour
I bid thee ask not half my realm for dower:
I dare not mock thy pure young soul; but say
How shall I honour—nought can thee repay?"
Thus spake the King to Cyra, as she stood
Before him trembling and with eyes subdued.
('Twas on the morn which saw the Palace cleared,
The guilty quelled, the lawful Sovereign feared.)
"Why tremble, child? Uplift to me the face
That met me first with smiles of infant grace,
Then when I saw it lie, a priceless gem
Shining in blood, all pleased, upturned to them
Who trode around thee, and had scorned to bow
To save from crushing hoofs thy radiant brow.
I saw, O God! thy bloody hands in play
Grasp at the fetlocks in their perilous way;
I seized thee up, around my neck were thrown
Thy little arms, and thou becam'st mine own.
With pride I reigned in youth: In those high days
Thy harp was filled with Zion's sorrowing lays:
Yea, yet a child, sweet wisdom was thy dower;
Thou saw'st my pride, and sang'st Jehovah's power,

Who for His people stretched His darkened hand,
And drove down wonders o'er the Egyptian land:
The green curled heaps of the curbed sea for them
The swift pursuing hosts of Pharaoh stem,
Heaved on them, whelming them; His Israel
O'er lands of drought and deserts terrible
He bore; before them went His cloud by day,
By night His fiery pillar led the way:
Such was thy anthem, such the argument,
That I might fear, for Judah might relent.
Dark dreams came o'er me; thy sweet soul refrained
From plaintive hymns, that I might not be pained:
Oh more than generous, delicately just
To sorrow wert thou when I lay in dust!
But I am raised to reason's awful peace;
And ne'er to tell thy goodness will I cease.
With songs the gifted bards of Babylon,
With harps peculiar, shall thy praise make known.
Aloft a golden tablet shall declare,
In grateful lines, for me thy wondrous care,
Reared on those mountains: Thee all lands shall know,
And in thy presence queens shall softly go."

With tears of gratitude the virgin kissed
The Monarch's hand, low kneeling to be blest.
"Be just," she rising said, "be more than kind
To me—let Zion's sufferings touch thy mind;
Build up her walls, her Temple! Let thy hand
Shield back our people to their ancient land!
Would that the days were come, oh would they were,
When old, old men again shall be in her,
Again forth leaning on their staves shall meet
With cheerful voices in each sunny street,
Shall count her towers, her later glories show,
Shall tell the praise of one exalted foe!

Think not of me, my young life's waning fast:
I feel it here. But oh, thy trouble's past!
And now, my King, my father, in my hour
Of death I'll claim of thee a daughter's dower:
Thy love alone from tears has kept me free,
When oft I've longed our sacred land to see;
Ne'er shall I see it, but I'll make thee swear
To take my body hence, and lay it there,
And wilt thou not, as in thy days of need
I've loved thee much? Thou wilt, thou wilt indeed!"

"I will not look; I'll hear thee not; nor speak,

As if my Cyra were so faint and sick!
Cold winds indeed have hurt thee in that den;
But fear not, God will make thee well again.
I'll talk of hope: 'Twere more to me than power,
To have thee near me to my latest hour;
Yet thee to honour, to myself severe,
I'll haste to set thee in a loftier sphere.
The prophet Daniel shares my council-board,
Young, beauteous, wise, accepted of the Lord;
Say, couldst thou love him? 'Twere a joy to me,
In raising him esteemed, to honour thee.
Then for his sake, for thine, would I restore
Thy people, make Jerusalem as before,
Make Daniel king; his spousal queen be thou,
And round to thee I'll make the kingdoms bow."

"No, no!" she said: "Restore our ancient race,
But let me die beholding still thy face!
Forgive me, Abraham's God!" She said, and grasped
And to her bosom passionately clasped
His knees, and sunk: One quick convulsive thrill
Throughout her body passed, and all was still.

II

He raised her up—O terror! O despair!
He pressed her heart—no pulse is stirring there.
Borne to a couch, he held that lovely head,
And gazed upon her in his silent dread;
By her unheeded now: No more she sees
Her father and her king—oh, more to her than these!
He started, called his slaves; but vain the aid
Of man, he closed the eyelids of the maid;
Then seized her lifeless hand: low bowing there,
He hid his face among her long black hair;
There lay through night, all silent in his woes;
And rose not up until the morn arose.

Canto VIII

The End Of Nebuchadnezzar

I

At morn the King arose: He bade be sought

Embalmers taught in Egypt; they were brought.
With linen pure and costly gums they dressed
That virgin body for the grave's long rest.

II

Within an ivory coffin Cyra lay;
Odorous lamps around her night and day
Burned, shining on her with a sweet dim light;
And there the Monarch fed his sorrowing sight.

Yet oft retired he, as he gave his leave
To Salem's princes o'er the maid to grieve.
Ezekiel heard and came; by Daniel's side
Walking, the Brethren in the Furnace tried
Came too; they stood around their daughter dead,
And lowly bowed was each majestic head.
Then communed they of Judah's earlier day,
Her prophet's vision, and her poet's lay,
Her judges, priests, her mighty men who fought
Jehovah's battles, and deliverance wrought;
Forgetting not those women famed of old,
For deeds beyond a woman's blood made bold.
Of Cyra then they spake, great was their praise
Of her endeavour Zion to upraise.
Then bowing down, when they had ceased to speak,
The sun of Buzi kissed the virgin's cheek,
Weeping the while. Forth from the place they go.
Back comes the King in his peculiar wo.

Long years—even till his death—his heart would there
Have kept her; but he rose from his despair;
Recalled her wish; and, greatly self-denied,
Ordained her body should not there abide,
But to Judea—such her last command—
Should go, should lie within her father's land.

Just to the dear departed one, he bade
Be chariots yoked, and horsemen swift arrayed,
At morn, a goodly escort, to convey
The honoured dead from Babylon away.
And in the tombs of Judah's princely race
Shall gentle Cyra have her burial-place:
Whate'er her birth, a praise with her she brings
More than the blood of many thronèd kings.

They come! they take her thence! Silent, aloof,

Stood the great King; then sought his Palace roof,
And saw that convoy darkly haste away
To Judah's land, beneath the western day.
Soft music mourned the while. On turrets stood,
On roofs and walls, the city's multitude,
All westward looking; thousand thousands laid
Their foreheads low for Cyra, honoured maid.
As for the King, he tore his straitened vest,
To ease the swelling trouble of his breast;
And watched that sable troop, till from his eyes,
Far fused to mist, the swimming vision dies.

III

Down walked the grief-struck King; but yet put on
A governed wo, and sate upon his throne:
His laws renewed, the glories of his State
Arranged, with god-like majesty he sate.

IV

Remembering then his pledge by Cyra won,
To raise her people up, the King bade this be done.
But grief for her already had subdued
His heart, relapsing to its mournful mood.
Quick drooped his life: the same revolving year
Saw Cyra die, and him upon his bier.
Yet held in honour their united name
Was Zion's helper, and deliverance came.

MONKWOOD

Part First

"I've done my work: o'er belts and breadths of earth,
Regions, and parallels, and wide degrees,
I've hunted him: I've done him down to death:
And his bones whiten in the wilderness.
Come, Grip."

He said, and rose, that lean dark man,
In umbered light, within his rocky cave,
And fed his brindled hound with gobbets raw.
The cloyed dog stretched and licked his bloody jaws,

And couched anew, his muzzle to the hearth.
Fresh logs the Master flung upon the fire,
Sputtering with sap; down then he sate, and eyed
The gulfy eddyings of the woolly smoke.

Far in the depths, rose on his shaping soul
A beauteous girl, and she came dancing on
Through the spring flowers before an antique hall,
Shaking her cloud of curls: not lightlier,
Translucent in the sunny dews of morn,
Dances the leaflet on the topmost twig.
And aye she smiled and nodded, coming near,
Nodding to him and smiling. Forward far,
As if to meet her, keen yet pleased of look,
Bending he sate.

Sudden he rose, he paced
The lurid cave; his eyes were balls of light;
But, ever as he turned him in his range,
Moister they gleamed:—"My sister, young and dear!
Gold, name it not; nor gems, seed of the sun!
All lustrous capable stones of mystery,
All rarest things of unconceived cost,
Take them all, all; give me my sister back,
As once she was, clear in her virgin dew!
What is she now?" He shuddered, down he sate,
And sitting brooded on the troubled Past.

What finds he there? His ancient house decayed,
His parents dead, his sister and himself
Grew up together, and were knit in one.
But proud from poverty, and all untrained
To equal duties, regular, mild, and safe,
Stern waxed young Monkwood: silently he spent
His hot impatience in the hunted woods.
To war he went. Betrayed, his sister fell;
But hid her shame among the Magdalens.

Monkwood has learnt it on the eve of fight.
Stern, still, wound up, he waited for that morn.
The morning came: the battle broke: outflew
His heart, uncoiling like a spring of steel:
Far leapt he dashing down that bloody gulf,
In terrible self-relief: a thousand deaths,
Ten thousand deaths were there; with open breast
He more than braved them all, he wooed them all,
That dreadful doer; but they passed him by,
And all unscathed with victory he stood.

Now then for honours on his noted head!
Away, away! farewell the pomp of war!
Hope, joy, farewell! His jealous soul has ta'en
His sister's blot, his family honour's blight,
Full on himself. Her he will see once more,
Once, and no more; vengeance he'll do her then
On her destroyer; then to home farewell—
His father's home! the wolfish solitudes
Of worlds afar, these be his fitting place,
To die at once, or eat his heart away.

In penitential depths, self-punishing,
His sister would not see him. In the Church
Of Magdalens he waited: from behind
The curtain of their sacred modesty,
Where all unseen they worshipped, there arose
The thankful song of the redeemed ones,
Swelling and thrilling: oh how Monkwood's soul
Yearned to untwist the symphony, and catch
His sister's separate voice! If in the low
And wailing fall of the relapsing hymn
Some heart-drawn lingering voice was left behind,
How he did drink it in!—" 'Tis she, 'tis she!
My lost, my found! I go, for I have heard,
More far to me than all the songs of time,
The uttered sorrow of thy contrite heart."

Now then for vengeance! for his natural man
Was unsubdued: Sheer down on him who slew
His sister's peace he bore: the villain fled,
But he pursued: o'er belts and breadths of earth,
Regions, and parallels, and wide degrees,
He hunted him; he did him down to death;
And his bones whiten in the wilderness.

His work of vengeance o'er, all moral hope
Of life exhausted, from the ways of men
Far vanished Monkwood in the Western world,
A salvage hunter of the homeless woods,
Lord of his cave, his rifle, and his dog.

Thus brooding sits he by his midnight fire,
His spirit ranging through that troubled Past.
Balm, is there none? The poppy, flower of fate,
Turning its milky eye to the ebon Land
Of Morpheus and of Dreams, grows round his cave,
Sown by him there; oft has it eased his heart,
But aye the wo returns with added wo.

What sunken lands forlorn, what sunless depths
Of rifted rocks, and blocked obstruction jammed,
Would he not search, if haply he might find
The Waters of Forgetfulness, and drink,
And wash his soul clean white of all the Past?

Lo! now he slumbers, red with ember gleams,
Couched on a spotted skin: The dreams come on:
The hollow roaring of Eternity
Is in his soul. What end of this despair?
Hope for him yet! the Angel of the Cross,
Who circles earth, on shores and desert isles,
Along the tracks of solitary men,
To sow the seed of light, has found him out,
Has tried his stubborn heart with fear and hope:
Waking, it yields not yet; in dreams by night
'Tis giving way. So let him dream! from out
That grisly struggle of his light and dark
May grow the gladness of the perfect day.

Part Second

Pride, wrath, revenge, the passions of his blood,
All dead; repentant o'er the pondered past,
And summing up the actions of the day,
Sits Father Monkwood by his evening fire.

Changed long ago, his worse than wasted youth
Filled him with sorrow; guided to the Cross,
He took its priestly training, and went forth
To give the solace which himself had found.
Strong-grained of good, as he had been of ill,
No danger daunted him, no trial stayed.
Lean with endeavour, through the Western world,
On to its outer rim, by watered plains,
And thankless sands; the stony drought of hills,
Glared down upon; plague-rotten swamps; the dusk
Of swarming forests; on by capes of ice
Horned to the floods; snow-wildered lands, far lands
Glimmering away into the skirts of time,
Lost at the Pole; all places, wheresoe'er
Were human hearts to suffer and to die,
There still was he with the immortal help.

Nor yet content with individual aims,
Widening of soul, with large prophetic eye,

He fixed the cradle of the coming Age
By fruitful rivers, measuring out for Man
The axe-doomed forests, and the virgin hills
Of mineral womb, the mothers yet to be
Of Iron Power, begot by Social Fire,
And cities sleeping in the shapeless stone,
All for the kingdom of the Lord of Life.

A sudden tempest tears the cracking night.
Uprising firm and slow, stately in age,
The Father from the entrance of his cave
Looks out and eyes, self-lit by its own fires,
Sucked through the mountain-gorges of the West,
The level havoc burst careering by.
Calm turning in he couches him to sleep,
Blessing the God who gives us in their change
The ordered seasons, and the day and night:—
Famine may waste, the blue spasmodic pest
May ride the tainted winds, with rifts may heave
The central fires, tilting the lifted hills,
And stony waves of movement undulate
Throughout the rock-ribbed earth; yet fear not, Man!
Upheld for Jesus' sake, this frame of things
Shall perish not until His own Great Day.
Plead thou the Incarnate Plea, and meet that Day,
Standing up calm before the Opened Books,
Tried in the last resort of wondering worlds.

THE OLD SOLDIER

Campaign The First

"Glory of War! But there—behold the end!"
The Old Soldier said: 'twas by his evening fire,
Winter the time: so saying, out he jerked
His wooden leg before him. With a look
Half comic, half pathetic, his gray head
Turned down askance, the pigtail out behind
Stiff with attention, saying nothing more,
He sat and eyed the horizontal peg.
Back home the stump he drew not, till with force
Disdainful deep into the slumbering fire
He struck the feruled toe, and poking roused
A cheery blaze, to light him at his work.
The unfinished skep is now upon his knee,
For June top-swarmers in his garden trim:

With twists of straw, and willow wattling thongs,
Crooning he wrought. The ruddy flickering fire
Played on his eyebrow shag, and thin fresh cheek,
Touching his varying eye with many a gleam.
His cot behind, soldierly clean and neat,
Gave back the light from many a burnished point,
His simple supper o'er, he reads The Book;
Then loads and mounts his pipe, puffing it slow,
Musing on days of yore, and battles old,
And many a friend and comrade dead and gone,
And vital ones, boughs of himself, cut off
From his dispeopled side, naked and bare.
Puffs short and hurried, puff on puff, betray
His swelling heart: up starts the Man, to keep
The Woman down: forth from his cot he views
Yon moon high going through the clouds of night,
Soft as the soul makes way through yielding dreams:
And Wonder listens in yon starry lofts.
No voice for him! True to the veins of blood,
His eyes still soften; turning in, he locks
His lonely door, and stumps away to bed.

Campaign The Second

How fresh the morning meadow of the Spring,
Pearl-seeded with the dew: adown its path,
Bored by the worms of night, the Old Soldier takes
His wonted walk, and drinks into his heart
The gush and gurgle of the cold green stream.
The huddled splendour of the April noon;
Glancings of rain; the mountain-tops all quick
With shadowy touches and with greening gleams;
Blue bent the Bow of God; the coloured clouds,
Soaked with the glory of the setting sun,—
These all are his for pleasure: his the Moon,
Chaste huntress, dipping, o'er the dewy hills,
Her silver buskin in the dying day.

The Summer morn is up: the tapering trees
Are all a-glitter. In his garden forth
The Old Soldado saunters: hovering on
Before him, oft upon the naked walk
Rests the red butterfly; now full dispread;
Now, in the wanton gladsomeness of life,
Half on their hinges folding up its wings;
Again full spread and still: o'erhead away,

Lo! now it wavers through the liquid blue.
But he intent from out their straw-roofed hives
Watches his little foragers go forth,
Boot on the buds to make, to suck the depths
Of honey-throated blooms, and home return,
Their thighs half smothered with the yellow dust.
Dibble and hoe he plies; anon he props
His heavy-headed plants, and visits round
His herbs of grace: the simple flowerets here
Open their infant buttons; there the flowers
Of preference blow, the lily and the rose.

Fast by his cottage door there grows an oak,
Of state supreme, drawn from the centuries.
Pride of the old man's heart, in many a walk
Far off he sees its top of sovereignty,
And with instinctive loyalty his cap
Soldierly touches to the Royal Tree—
King of all trees that flourish! King revered!
Trafalgars lie beneath his rugged vest,
And in his acorns is the Golden Age!
Summer the time; thoughtful beneath his tree
The Veteran puffs his intermittent pipe,
And cheats the sweltering hours; yet noting oft
The flight of bird, and exhalation far
Quivering and drifting o'er the fallow field,
And the great cloud rising upon the noon,
The sultry smithy of the thunder-forge.
Anon the weekly journal of events
Conning, he learns the doings of the world,
And what it suffers—justice-loosened wrath
Falling from Heaven upon unrighteous states;
Lean Sorrow tracking still the bread-blown Sin;
A spirit of lies; high-handed wrong; the curse
Of ignorance crass and fat stupidity;
And maddened nations at their contre-dance
Of Revolutions, when each bloody hour
Comes staggering in beneath its load of crimes,
Enough to bend the back of centuries.

The sun goes down the western afternoon,
Lacing the clouds with his diverging rays:
Homeward the children from the village school
Come whooping on; but aye their voices fall,
As aye they turn unto the old man's door—
So much they love him. He their progress notes
In learning, and has prizes for their zeal,
Flowers for the girls, and fruit,—hooks for the boys,

Whistles, and cherry-stones; and, to maintain
The thews and sinews of our coming men,
He makes them run and leap upon the green.

The nodding wain has borne the harvest home,
And yellowing apples spot the orchard trees:
Now may you oft the Old Soldado see
Stumping, relieved against the evening sky,
Along the ferny height—so much he loves
Its keen and wholesome air; nor less he loves
To hear the rustling of the fallen leaves,
Swept by the wind along the glittering road,
As home he goes beneath the Autumnal moon.

Thus round the starry girdle of the year
His spirit circles thankfully. Not grieved
When Winter comes once more, his hale red cheek
Goes kindling through the cold, forth when the morn
Tinkles with ice, and when on day's far edge,
Down in the windy trouble of the west,
Night's ghostly masons build the toppling clouds.

Zest to his cottage thus: with chosen books
He sits with Wisdom by his evening fire;
Puff goes his cheerful pipe; by turns he works;
And ever from his door, before he sleeps,
He eyes the sister planets, luminous large,
Silent, soft spinning on their mystic wheels
The thread of time: how beautiful they be!

Campaign The Third

Lo! yonder sea-mew seeks the inland moss:
Beautiful bird! how snowy clean it shows
Behind the ploughman, on a glinting day,
Trooping with rooks, and farther still relieved
Against the dark-brown mould, alighting half,
Half hovering still; yet far more beautiful
Its glistening sleekness, when from out the deep
Sudden and shy emerging on your lee,
What time thro' breeze, and spray, and freshening brine,
Your snoring ship, beneath her cloud of sail,
Bends on her buried side, carried it rides
The green curled billow and the seething froth,
Turning its startled head this way and that,
Half looking at you with its wild blue eye,

Then moves its fluttering wings and dives anew!

Smoking his pipe of peace, wearing away
The summer eve, the Old Soldado sits
Beneath his buzzing oak, and eyes the bird,
With many a thought of the suggested sea.
The veering gull came circling back and near:
"What! nearer still?" the Veteran said, and rose,
And doffed his bonnet, and held down his pipe:
"Give me her message, then! Oh, be to me
Her spirit not unconscious from the deep
Of how I mourn her loss! Bird, ah! you're gone.
Vain dreamer I! For every night my soul
Knocks at the gates of the invisible world;
But no one answers me, no little hand
Comes out to grasp at mine. Well, all is good:
Even, bird, thy heart-deceiving change of flight,
To teach me patience, was ordained of old."

Yes, all is ordered well: Aimless may seem
The wandering foot; even it commissioned treads
The very lines by Providence laid down,
Sure, though unseen, of all-converging good:
Look up, old man, and see:—

Along the road
Came one in sailor's garb: his shallow hat
Of glazed and polished leather shone like tin.
A fair young damsel led him by the hand—
For he was blind: and to the summer sun,
Fearless and free, he held his bronzèd face.
An armless sleeve, pinned to his manly breast,
Told he had been among the "Hearts of Oak."
The damsel saw the old man of the tree,
His queue of character, and wooden leg,
And smiling whispered to the tar she led.
Near turned, both stood. Down from her shoulder then
The maid unslung a mandolin, and played,
High singing as she played, a battle-piece
Of bursts and pauses: keeping time the while,
Now furious fast, now dying slow away,
His pigtail wagging with emotion deep,
The Old Soldier puffed his sympathetic pipe.
The minstrel ceased; he drew his leathern purse,
With pension lined, and offered guerdon due.
"Nay," said the maiden, smiling, "for your tye
Alone I played, and for your wooden leg;
Yea, but for these, the symbols of the things

You've done and suffered—like my father here."

"Well, then, you'll taste my honey and my bread?"
The Soldier said, and from his cot he brought
Seats for the strangers; him the damsel helped,
Bearing the bread and honey; and they ate,
The damsel serving, and she ate in turn.
When various talk had closed the simple feast,
The strangers rose to go: "My head! my head!"
The sailor cried, and fell in sudden pangs.
They bore and laid him on the Soldier's bed.
Forth ran the lass, and from the neighbouring town
Brought the physician; but all help was vain,
For God had touched him, and the man must die.
His mind was clear: "Give me that cross, my child,
That I may kiss it ere my spirit part,"
He said. And from her breast the damsel drew
A little cross, peculiar shaped and wrought,
And gave it him. It caught the Soldier's eye;
And when the girl received it back, he took
And looked at it.

"This cross, O dying man,
Was round my daughter's neck, when in the deep
She perished from me, on that fatal night
The 'Sphinx' was burnt, forth sailing from the Clyde.
Her dying mother round the infant's neck
This holy symbol, with her blessing, hung.
Friendless at home, I took my only child,
Bound to the Western World, where we had friends.
Scarce out of port, up flamed our ship on fire,
With crowding terrors through the umbered night.
Oh what a shout of joy, when through the gloom
Which walled us round within our glaring vault,
Spectral and large, we saw the ship of help!
Our boats were lowered; the first, o'ercrowded, swamped;
Down to the second, as it lurched away,
I flung my child: the monstrous waves went by
With backs like blood: the sudden-shifting boat
Is off with one, another has my babe.
I sprung to save her—all the rest is drear
Grisly confusion, till I found me laid,
In some far island, in a fisher's hut.
Me, as they homeward scudded past the fire,
Those lonely farmers of the deep picked up,
Floating away, and rubbed to vital heat;
And through the fever-gulf which had me next,
With simple love they brought my weary life.

The shores and islands round, for lingering news
Of people saved from off that burning wreck,
Oh how I haunted then; but of my child
No man had heard. Hopeless, and naked poor,
I rushed to war: from zone to zone, across
The rifts of ice, beneath the strokes of heat,
Reckless I fought. This cot received me next;
And here, I trust, my mortal chapter ends.
But say, oh say, how came you by this cross?"

The dying man had risen upon his arm,
Ere ceased the Soldier's tale: "She is thy child,
Take her," he said; "and may she be to thee,
As she to me has been, a daughter true,
A child of good, a blessing from on high!"
So saying, back he fell. Around his neck
Her arms of love the sobbing damsel threw,
And kissed him many a time. And then she rose,
And flung herself upon the Soldier's breast—
For he's her father too. And many tears,
Silent, the old man rained upon her neck.

"O wondrous hour!" the dying tar went on,
"Who could have thought of this! I am content.
The Lord be praised that she has found a friend,
Since I must go from her! That night of fire,
Our brig of war bore down upon your ship,
And sent her boats to save you from the flame.
Near you we could not come; so forth I swam,
And to your crowded stern I fixed a rope,
To take the people off. Back as I slid
Along the line to show them how to come,
A child, upheaved upon the billow top,
Was borne against my breast; I snatched her up;
Fast to my neck she clung; none could I find
To claim and take her: she was thus mine own.
That night she wore the cross which now she wears.
Why need I tell the changes of my life?
In war I lost an arm, and then an eye;
My other eye went out from sympathy,
And home I came a blind and helpless man.
But I had still one comforter, my child—
My young breadwinner, too! From wake to wake
She led me on, playing her mandolin,
Which I had brought her from the south of Spain.
She'll tell you all the rest when I am gone.
Bury me now in your own burial-place,
That still our daughter may be near my dust.

And Jesus keep you both!" He said, and died.

They buried him in their own burial-place.
And many a flower, heart-planted by that maid,
And good Old Soldier, bloomed upon his grave.
And many a requiem, when the gloaming came,
The damsel played above his honoured dust.
Not less, but all the more, her heart was knit
Unto her own true father. He, the while,
How proud was he to give her up his keys,
Mistress installed of all his little stores;
And introduce her to his flowers, and bees,
Making the sea-green honey—all for her;
And sit beside her underneath the oak,
Listening the story of her bygone life.
In turn she made him of her mother tell,
And aye a tear dropped on her needlework;
And all his wars the old campaigner told.
And God was with them, and in peace and love
They dwelt together in their happy home.

A FATHER'S CURSE: A DREAM, IN FOUR VISIONS

Vision First

A widowed father from the holy fount
Of Christian sprinkling bore his first-born babe
Home through the Sabbath noon. And aye his hand
Arranged the garment in a lighter fold
To overshade that breathing face upturned,
Yet let it freely drink the vital air.
And oft scarce walked he in his gaze intent,
Which fed on his boy's face,
Come out of his own loins,
Formed in the painful side
Of a dear mother—gone to barren dust.
O the wet violets of those sleeping eyes,
Which glisten through their silky fringèd lids!
Look to that dimpled smile! Look to those gums,
How sweet they laugh! His little features change,
To fear now fashioned in his baby dreams:
With many a kiss and many a murmured word,
Fain would that father chase away the shadow!

The Sabbath sun went down the western day.

His sloping beam, mingled with coloured motes,
Came through the leafy checkered lattice in,
Passing into a little bed of peace,
Where lay, in vestments white of innocence,
That child of many vows; no ruder sound
Than chirp of lonely sparrow in the thatch,
Or fluttering wing of butterfly which beat
The sunny pane, to break his slumber calm.
Before him near, in that mild solemn light,
Kneeling his father prayed.

Vision Second

The Bow was on the East:
One horn descending on a snow-white flock
Of lambs at rest upon a sleek hill-side,
The other showered its saffron and its blue
Down on a band of young girls in the vale,
Tossing their ringlets in their linkèd dance,
Laughing and winking to the glimmering sheen:
Through them and over them the glory fell,
Into the emerald meadow bending inward.
Beneath its arch,
Of beauty built, of promise, and of safety,
I saw that father as a woodman go;
And wide behind him ran his little boy.
They reached a woody gallery of hills,
And there that father felled the lofty trees,
Whose rustling leaves shook down their twinkling drops,
Wetting his clear axe, glittering in the sun.
Perversely sate aloof, and turned away,
Nor gratified his parent with attention
To what he did, with questions all between,
That boy among the ferns, intently fixed,
Plaiting a crown of rushes white and green.
He tore it with fierce glee.
He tore his flowerets, gathered as he came,
Wildings of coloured summer, heeding ne'er
The freaks and fancies in their spotted cups.
The young outglancing arrows of his eye
Were tipped with cruel pleasure, as he sprung
With froward shoutings leaping through the wood,
O'er shadows lying on the dewy grass,
Hunting a dragon-fly with shivering wings.
The wild-bees swinging in the bells of flowers,
Sucking the honeyed seeds with murmurs hoarse,

Were crushed to please him, for that fly escaped.
The callow hedgelings chirping through the briar
He caught, and tore their fluttering little wings;
Then hied to where came down a sunless glade,
Cold tinkling waters through the soft worn earth,
Never sun-visited, but when was seen
His green and yellow hair from out the west
Thro' thinner trees, spun 'twixt the fresh broad leaves—
But ne'er it warmed the ground, bare save where tufts
Of trailing plants for ever wet and cold,
And tender stools of slippery fungi grew:
There in a sweet pellucid pool, that boy
Drowned the young birds of summer one by one.
Back came he near his father,
Yet to him turned not; whistling, looking round
To see what farther mischief he could do;
Then laid him down and dug into the ground.
Oft turned to him the while
His father fondly looked: Heart-crowding thoughts
Of boyhood's growing wants, and coming youth,
Strengthened a parent's loins: faint shall they not,
Strong for his son shall be: forth shall he tread
The summer slope, the winter's dun green hill
Where melting hail is mingled with the grass,
To strike the gnarled elbows of the oaks.
Now, as he turned renewed unto his toil,
His bosom swelled into the heavèd stroke.
The self-willed boy,
Perversely angry that his father spake not,
And holding in his heart a contest with him,
Formed by himself, of coldness best sustained,
Refrained no longer, but looked round in spite:
He saw the sunbeam through the pillared trees
Fall on his father's bald and polished head,
Bowing and rising to the labouring axe;
Mouth, eye, and finger mocked that father's head!

Vision Three

There stood a ruined house!
In days of other years, perchance, within
Were beds of sleep, bread, and the sacred hearth,
Children, and joy, and sanctifying grief,
A mother's lessons, and a father's prayers.
Where now that good economy of life?
Scattered throughout the earth?

Or has it burst its bounds,
And left this broken outer shell,
Swelling away into the eternal worlds?
The path to the weed-mantled well grows green;
The swallow builds among the sooty rafters,
Low flying out and in through the dashed window.

Throughout the livelong day
No form of life comes here,
Save now and then a beggar sauntering by
The stumps, wool-tufted, of the old worn hedge,
That scarcely marks where once a garden was:
He, as he turns the crazy gate, and stops,
Seeing all desolate, then comes away
Muttering, seems cheerless sad
Beyond his daily wants.
No sound of feet
Over that threshold now is heard,
Save when on bleak October eve,
The cold and cutting wind, which blows all through
The hawthorn-bush, ruffling the blue hedge-sparrow,
Shivers the little neat-herd boy beneath,
Nestling to shun the rain
That hits his flushed cheek with sore-driving drops,
And forces him to seek those sheltering walls,
Low running with bent head: But soon the awe
Of things gone by, and the wood-eating worm—
To him the death-tick—drives him forth again
Beneath the scudding blast.
There came an old man leaning on his staff,
And bowing went into that ruined house:
It was that father!
This was the home to which he brought his bride:
This was the home where his young wife had died:
This was the home where he had reared his boy.
Forth soon he came;
And many tears fell from his aged eyes
Down to the borders of his trembling garment.
Who comes? He shrinks away; he fears to meet
That man, his son! Bold strokes had made him rich:
And, vain not kind, he to a showy dwelling
Had ta'en his father from that lowly cot.
Yet there the old man totters; there those walls
Stand, what but record of his own mean birth?
He swept those walls away.

An old old man sate near a lordly house,
Trembling, not daring once to lift his eyes

Even to the speckled linnet on the bush:
'Twas he—that father!
Came sweeping silks, a haughty pair went past:
That proud disdainful fellow is his son;
And she who leans upon his arm, attired
With impudence, his wife, whose wealth has made
Him higher still, both heedless of their father.

Vision Fourth

That father died neglected, and in death
With struggling love were mingled bitter thoughts—
A Father's Curse.
This, ere his head went down into the grave,
Dug in a corner where meek strangers lie,
Had upward sprung, a messenger succinct,
To trouble all the crystal range of Heaven,
To call on Hell, to post o'er seas and lands,
Nature to challenge in her last domain,
Not to let pass the accursed.
I here came a voice—it cried,
"The storms are ready."
Forth flew into mid air that Father's form,
No longer mean, a potentate of wrath,
To rule the elements and set them on.

He called the Storms—they came;
He pointed to his son:
There stood that son—no wife was with him now,
No children pleaded for his naked head—
Upon a broken hill, abrupt and strange,
Under a sky which darkened to a twilight;
A huddled world of woods and waters crushed,
Hung tumbling round him, earthquake-torn and jammed
From Nature's difficult throes: cut off he stood
From ways of men, from mercy, and from help,
With chasms and ramparts inaccessible.
The tree-tops streaming toward his outcast head,
Showed that the levelled winds smote sore on him;
Gaunt rampant monsters, half-drawn from the woods,
Roared at him glaring; downward on his eyes
The haggard vulture was in act to swoop;
Rains plashed on him; hail hit him; darting down,
The flaming forks blue quivered round him keen,
And many thunders lifted up their voice:
All Nature was against him.

Out leapt a bolt,
And split the mount beneath his sinking feet.
O'er him his Father's form burnt fiercely red,
Nearer and nearer still,
Dislimned and fused into one sheeted blaze.
From out it fell a bloody drizzled shower,
Rained on that bad son's head descending fast,
Terror thereon aghast—he's down! he's gone!
Darkness has swallowed up the scene convulsed.

www.ingramcontent.com/pod-product-compliance
Lightning Source LLC
Chambersburg PA
CBHW021946040426
42448CB00008B/1257